A kid's journal to record their nature experiences.
Includes nature facts, games, experiments,
crafts and ways to help the earth!

This NatureLog belongs to:

Special thanks to:
Nature's Creator!
My parents for nurturing my creative drive
My husband, Peter for being "the rock"
My children, Michael and Daniel who inspired this book

20 19 18 17 16 15 14 13 12 11

ISBN: 978-1-885061-54-6

Published by Adventure Publications
An imprint of AdventureKEEN
820 Cleveland Street South
Cambridge, Minnesota 55008
(800) 678-7006
www.adventurepublications.net

Printed and bound in China

Cover and interior design/illustration:
DeAnna Brandt
Copy: Laura Holte and DeAnna Brandt

Notice: The information contained in
this book is true, complete, and
accurate to the best of our knowledge.
All recommendations and suggestions
are made without any guarantees on
the part of the author or Adventure
Publications.
The author and publisher
disclaim all liability incurred in
connection with the use of this
information. Neither the publisher nor
the author shall be liable for any
damage which may be caused or
sustained as a result of the conduct
of any of the activities in this book.

Log Tips

Record It!

As you explore the natural world around you, write down on the "Log" pages any critters or plants that you notice.

Respect Nature!

Please leave things as you find them. Leave any eggs or babies in their nests or homes, do not pick leaves off trees, if you turn over a log or stone to see what's underneath, put it back carefully when you're done. Keep these guidelines in mind as you explore!

Look Closely!

Your "Observations" may include: what is its color, size, shape, body covering (feathers, fur, scales, etc)? Does it make a noise? Does it have an odor?

Look Even Closer!

What is it doing? How does it move (walk/jump/fly/swim/ not move)? How many are there? Are there any tracks? Is there a nest or home? Are there any babies or eggs? What else is interesting? What are the weather conditions?

Check It Out!

You may want to look your critter or plant up in a nature book or field guide to find out more about it.

Be Creative!

Use the "Notes/Photos/Art pages to paste in a picture that you've drawn or a photograph you've taken or a magazine picture you have cut out (with permission)! A postcard would work too! Or, you may wish to use the space to write down more information, glue pressed flowers, a leaf or even a feather!

Have Fun!

Learn more with the nature "Facts" and have fun with the "Try Its" (experiments and crafts). The "Games" are easy and can be done almost any-where. Give back to nature with the ideas in the "Helps" sections.

Other Uses!

Use this NatureLog at the zoo, natural history museum, science museum, or while watching a movie or television show about nature.

Quick Log

Use this page as a summary of all the items
you have recorded in this NatureLog

	Date	Critter/Plant
1		
2		
3		
4		
5		
6		
7		
8		
9		
10		
11		
12		
13		
14		
15		
16		
17		
18		
19		
20		
21		
22		
23		

Quick Log

Use this page as a summary of all the items
you have recorded in this NatureLog

	Date	Critter/Plant
24		
25		
26		
27		
28		
29		
30		
31		
32		
33		
34		
35		
36		
37		
38		
39		
40		
41		
42		
43		
44		
45		
46		

Log

What I saw: _____

Date: _____

Where I saw it: _____

Observations: _____

_____

_____

_____

_____

_____

_____

_____

_____

It looked like this:

Fact

The elephant, weighing in at six tons, is the heaviest mammal on land.

The giraffe is the tallest at 17 feet, and the cheetah is the fastest, racing at 60 miles per hour.

Mammals are warm-blooded, have fur or hair on their bodies, feed their young milk, and have a unique type of jawbone.

Try it

Growing art!

Put a damp napkin on a dish.

Place some seeds on the napkin in the shape of a face, heart, your name, etc.

Remember to keep the napkin slightly wet and warm.

As the days pass, watch your artwork come alive!

What I saw: _____

Date: _____

Where I saw it: _____

Observations: _____

_____

_____

_____

_____

_____

_____

_____

_____

It looked like this:

Log

What I saw: _____

Date: _____

Where I saw it: _____

Observations: _____

_____

_____

_____

_____

_____

_____

_____

It looked like this:

Game

Leaf Races:
Two or more
people each
put a leaf on a
paper plate and
put the plate on
their heads.

Then race
(walk?) to
a finish line
with the leaf
and plate
still on the
racer's head.

Vary the game
by using a
blade of grass,
milkweed, a
feather or
dandelion on
the plate.

Fact

Hummingbirds can flap their wings up to 80 times every second!

The ruby-throated hummningbird can fly 500 miles non-stop in crossing the Gulf of Mexico.

What I saw: _____

Date: _____

Where I saw it: _____

Observations: _____

_____

_____

_____

_____

_____

_____

_____

_____

It looked like this:

6

Log

What I saw: _____

Date: _____

Where I saw it: _____

Observations: _____

_____

_____

_____

_____

_____

_____

_____

_____

It looked like this:

Fact

Owls swallow their prey whole.

Instead of digesting the bones, beaks, fur, or feet, the owl coughs up the remains in the form of pellets.

Look for them at the base of trees under where an owl might perch.

Try it

In a forest, meadow or park, sit or lie down on your back with both fists on your stomach.

Every time you hear a new bird song, lift one finger.

See how many different bird songs you hear in 10 minutes.

Vary the game by listening for any animal sounds - or any sounds at all, like wind, leaves, water.

What I saw: _____

Date: _____

Where I saw it: _____

Observations: _____

_____

_____

_____

_____

_____

_____

_____

_____

It looked like this:

Notes / Photos / Art

Notes / Photos / Art

Log

What I saw: _____

Date: _____

Where I saw it: _____

Observations: _____

_____

_____

_____

_____

_____

_____

_____

_____

It looked like this:

"Adopt" a piece of the earth.

Walk around your yard and find an area that needs attention (it may be a place that has no plants on it or is littered).

Some ideas: plant some seeds to save the soil, hang a bird feeder on a pole to give birds food year-round, pick up any litter.

Fact

A pocket gopher's front teeth, like those of other rodents, never stop growing.

They grow up to 15 inches in a year.

Constant chewing and gnawing wears them down so they remain the same size.

What I saw: _____

Date: _____

Where I saw it: _____

Observations: _____

_____

_____

_____

_____

_____

_____

_____

_____

_____

It looked like this:

Log

What I saw: _____

Date: _____

Where I saw it: _____

Observations: _____

_____

_____

_____

_____

_____

_____

_____

_____

It looked like this:

Fact

A bloodhound's sense of smell can be up to one million times sharper than a human's.

For this reason bloodhounds have been bred for tracking.

They can even find the almost invisible pieces of skin shed from a moving person's body.

Try it

Worker bees can sometimes travel up to 8 miles to a plentiful bunch of flowers carrying with them up to half their body weight in nectar.

Weigh yourself and figure out half your body weight.

Find something of that weight and try carrying it - could you go 8 miles?

What I saw: _____

Date: _____

Where I saw it: _____

Observations: _____

_____

_____

_____

_____

_____

_____

_____

_____

_____

It looked like this:

Log

What I saw: _____

Date: _____

Where I saw it: _____

Observations: _____

_____

_____

_____

_____

_____

_____

_____

_____

It looked like this:

Game

Have one person go into the yard, forest or park and fill a small bag with items from the ground (a twig, pinecone, leaf, rock, acorn, etc.) without the other person watching.

Now, the other person, without looking, puts their hand in the bag and tries to identify each item by touch alone.

Gather new items and reverse players.

15

Fact

One of the heaviest animals on land is the hippopotamus, which can weigh more than three tons.

Hippos spend the day wallowing in mud or soaking in rivers or lakes with only their eyes, ears, and nostrils above water.

They come onto land at night to eat grass near the water's edge.

What I saw: _____

Date: _____

Where I saw it: _____

Observations: _____

_____

_____

_____

_____

_____

_____

_____

_____

_____

It looked like this:

Notes / Photos / Art

Notes / Photos / Art

Log

What I saw: _____

Date: _____

Where I saw it: _____

Observations: _____

_____

_____

_____

_____

_____

_____

_____

_____

It looked like this:

Try it

Gently put a worm on a piece of moist paper and watch how it uses its muscles to move.

Put your ear close to the paper and listen.

You will be able to hear the scratching sound of the bristles on the underside of its body that grab the surface as it moves.

Gently put the worm back where you found it.

What I saw: _____

Date: _____

Where I saw it: _____

Observations: _____

_____

_____

_____

_____

_____

_____

_____

_____

_____

It looked like this:

Log

What I saw: _____

Date: _____

Where I saw it: _____

Observations: _____

_____

_____

_____

_____

_____

_____

_____

_____

It looked like this:

Help

Call the local humane society or animal shelter and ask if there are any one-time volunteer tasks they need help with.

With an adult, discuss which one(s) you can do.

If this works out, consider helping out on a regular basis.

If you decide to get a pet, check these kinds of places first – there might be one that's just right for you.

Fact

Wolves are very protective of pups in their pack.

Many pack members will take turns standing guard over the pups.

If the mother must leave to get food, another adult will "babysit" the pups for her.

What I saw: _____

Date: _____

Where I saw it: _____

Observations: _____

_____

_____

_____

_____

_____

_____

_____

_____

It looked like this:

Log

What I saw: _____

Date: _____

Where I saw it: _____

Observations: _____

_____

_____

_____

_____

_____

_____

_____

It looked like this:

Try it

How old is the tree?

Use some string or a tape measure to measure around different trees about 3 feet above the ground.

Species vary, but generally, one year's growth equals about one inch.

Compare the heights of any trees that measure the same around its trunk – they are about the same age.

Log

What I saw: _____

Date: _____

Where I saw it: _____

Observations: _____

_____

_____

_____

_____

_____

_____

_____

_____

It looked like this:

Notes / Photos / Art

Notes / Photos / Art

Log

What I saw: _____

Date: _____

Where I saw it: _____

Observations: _____

_____

_____

_____

_____

_____

_____

_____

_____

It looked like this:

Game

With two or more people, pin or tape a picture of an animal on the back of one person without letting him see it.

The person with the picture can ask only yes/no questions to try and guess what animal it is.

Fact

Ant facts:
There are at
least 14,000
different kinds
of ants.

Except for the
polar regions,
ants are found
everywhere
on land.

Ants have the
longest life
span of any
insect—an
average of
eight years.

Ants can lift
up to 50 times
their own
body weight.

What I saw: _____

Date: _____

Where I saw it: _____

Observations: _____

_____

_____

_____

_____

_____

_____

_____

_____

It looked like this:

Log

What I saw: _____

Date: _____

Where I saw it: _____

Observations: _____

_____

_____

_____

_____

_____

_____

_____

_____

_____

It looked like this:

Fact

You can identify the type of ladybug by the number of spots it has (if any), but spots do not indicate age.

Ladybugs are popular insects with humans because they are excellent pest controllers.

Many eat aphids, white flies and other bugs that damage garden plants.

29

Try it

Draw pictures of animals on 3x5 cards, one per card.

Cut each animal in half from top to bottom.

Put the top or front half of one animal with the back or bottom half of another.

What kinds of critters can you invent?

A girphant (half giraffe, half elephant)?, a lizpillar (half lizard, half caterpillar)?

What I saw: _____

Date: _____

Where I saw it: _____

Observations: _____

_____

_____

_____

_____

_____

_____

_____

_____

It looked like this:

Log

What I saw: _____

Date: _____

Where I saw it: _____

Observations: _____

_____

_____

_____

_____

_____

_____

_____

_____

It looked like this:

Help

Next time you visit the beach or the park, take along a large and a small garbage bag.

Try to fill the large one with trash that you find.

Close it up and throw it in a garbage can.

Use the small one for any aluminum cans or glass you may find and bring them to the nearest recycling containers.

Fact

Only the females in ants, wasps and bees sting.

The only bee that dies once it stings is the honey bee.

The tiny barbs on its stinger get stuck in your skin.

The bee's abdomen usually rips off and the bee dies when it tries to pull the stinger out.

What I saw: _____

Date: _____

Where I saw it: _____

Observations: _____

_____

_____

_____

_____

_____

_____

_____

_____

It looked like this:

Notes / Photos / Art

Notes / Photos / Art

MOOSE

Log

What I saw: _____

Date: _____

Where I saw it: _____

Observations: _____

_____

_____

_____

_____

_____

_____

_____

_____

It looked like this:

Fact

Fish grow throughout their lives.

The number of scales on a fish stay the same, the scales just get bigger as the fish grows.

Growth rings are formed on the scales and from them you can calculate the age of the fish.

Try it

Take a (mini) hike!

Make a circle with a 5' piece of string and lay it down on an interesting piece of ground.

With or without a magnifying glass, lay down and "hike" on your belly looking at the various wonders: beetles with powerful jaws, grass blades bent by dew, a baby spider scrambling for cover, etc.

Log

What I saw: _____

Date: _____

Where I saw it: _____

Observations: _____

_____

_____

_____

_____

_____

_____

_____

_____

It looked like this:

Log

What I saw: _____

Date: _____

Where I saw it: _____

Observations: _____

_____

_____

_____

_____

_____

_____

_____

_____

It looked like this:

Game:

Nature Scavenger Hunt.

With 2 or more people make a list of things to collect from your yard, park or woods and then go find them.

Some ideas: a feather, 50 of something, a bone, 3 different seeds, something white, some- thing fuzzy, something straight, something sharp.

Return these items safely, without damage.

37

Fact

Blue whales are the largest and heaviest animals on earth.

They grow up to 100 feet long—larger than the dinosaurs.

They weigh 150 tons—about the same as 2,000 people.

These whales can live to be 80 years old.

What I saw: _____

Date: _____

Where I saw it: _____

Observations: _____

_____

_____

_____

_____

_____

_____

_____

_____

It looked like this:

Log

What I saw: _____

Date: _____

Where I saw it: _____

Observations: _____

_____

_____

_____

_____

_____

_____

_____

_____

It looked like this:

Fact

To protect its eggs, the cichlid fish, found in African lakes, keep the eggs inside its mouth.

The young swim out when they hatch, then return to the parents' mouth for safety.

Try it

Have someone blindfold you and carefully bring you to a spot in your yard, in the woods, or a park.

Explore your surroundings until you know the spot well.

Then, still blindfolded, have them bring you to another spot somewhat close by, then remove the blindfold.

Now try to find the place you just explored!

What I saw: _____

Date: _____

Where I saw it: _____

Observations: _____

_____

_____

_____

_____

_____

_____

_____

_____

_____

It looked like this:

Notes / Photos / Art

Notes / Photos / Art

Log

What I saw: _____

Date: _____

Where I saw it: _____

Observations: _____

_____

_____

_____

_____

_____

_____

_____

_____

It looked like this:

Help

Trees give us paper, fruit, nuts, lumber, living spaces for animals and birds and keep our air clean.

You can help by planting one.

Visit the local nursery or garden center with your mom or dad.

Figure out which type of tree would work best for your location considering soil type, light and space.

Plant it and take care of it – watch it grow!

Fact

Use this general rule of thumb to identify common frogs and toads:

Frogs are moist and slimy, and with long hind legs, can jump surprising distances.

Toads are dry and warty and with stout bodies and short legs, can only hop short distances.

(No, you cannot get warts from holding either toads or frogs!)

44

What I saw: _____

Date: _____

Where I saw it: _____

Observations: _____

_____

_____

_____

_____

_____

_____

_____

_____

_____

It looked like this:

Log

What I saw: _____

Date: _____

Where I saw it: _____

Observations: _____

_____

_____

_____

_____

_____

_____

_____

_____

_____

It looked like this:

Fact

Amphibians, found everywhere but Antarctica and Greenland, have been around for millions of years.

They are able to live both on land and in the water.

Amphibians are a class of vertebrates that include frogs, toads, salamanders, newts, and caecilians (an animal from tropical regions that has no limbs).

Try it

Blindfold a friend and carefully lead them to a tree.

Ask them to get to know details of the tree by feeling it.

How big around is it?

Does it have a special bump, hole, smell?

Lead your friend away from that tree and remove the blindfold.

Can they find the tree they just explored?

What I saw: _____

Date: _____

Where I saw it: _____

Observations: _____

_____

_____

_____

_____

_____

_____

_____

_____

It looked like this:

Log

What I saw: _____

Date: _____

Where I saw it: _____

Observations: _____

_____

_____

_____

_____

_____

_____

_____

_____

_____

It looked like this:

Game

From the ground, gather about 20 or 30 somewhat straight twigs.

Holding them about 2 feet above the ground, let them fall.

Taking turns, one person tries to pick up a twig without moving any others.

If they succeed, they get to try again.

You may use a "rescued" twig as a tool to get another.

47

Fact

Turtles vary greatly in size.

The leatherback turtle is the largest of the turtles.

The average adult grows to about 6 ft. long and weighs about 1,000 lbs.

The common mud turtle is only 3 to 5 in. long.

Sea turtles are the fastest swimmers, racing along at up to 20 mph.

What I saw: _____

Date: _____

Where I saw it: _____

Observations: _____

_____

_____

_____

_____

_____

_____

_____

_____

It looked like this:

Notes / Photos / Art

Notes / Photos / Art

Log

What I saw: _____

Date: _____

Where I saw it: _____

Observations: _____

_____

_____

_____

_____

_____

_____

_____

_____

It looked like this:

Fact

By sticking out their tongues, snakes detect smells in the air.

Odors in the air stick to fluid on the snake's flicking tongue and are drawn into its mouth.

Using its tongue, a snake can steer clear of danger, follow prey, or seek a mate.

Try it

The next time you go for a walk, scrape the mud from the bottom of your shoes into a dish of black dirt or potting soil.

Keep it moist and in the sun.

In about 6-8 days you'll find out if you helped any seeds to spread!

What I saw: _____

Date: _____

Where I saw it: _____

Observations: _____

_____

_____

_____

_____

_____

_____

_____

_____

_____

It looked like this:

Log

What I saw: _____

Date: _____

Where I saw it: _____

Observations: _____

_____

_____

_____

_____

_____

_____

_____

_____

It looked like this:

Help

Call your place of worship or local food shelter and ask what types of food or supplies they donate to those in need.

With some of your allowance, gift, or chore money, buy some of these items the next time you go to shopping and bring the items to donate.

Fact

Fish sleep with their eyes open because they have no eyelids.

They often rest on the bottom or near water plants.

The parrotfish spends almost an hour each evening wrapping itself in a blanket of mucus before going to sleep.

Log

What I saw: _____

Date: _____

Where I saw it: _____

Observations: _____

_____

_____

_____

_____

_____

_____

_____

_____

It looked like this:

Log

What I saw: _____

Date: _____

Where I saw it: _____

Observations: _____

_____

_____

_____

_____

_____

_____

_____

_____

It looked like this:

Try it

Pick up some leaves from the ground that have large veins and ribs.

Paint the vein side of one leaf with a thin layer of paint.

Press the leaf onto a clean sheet of paper and gently rub it being careful not to move the leaf.

Peel the leaf away and let it dry.

Write a letter to a friend or print more leaves in other colors on the same paper and frame it.

What I saw: _____

Date: _____

Where I saw it: _____

Observations: _____

_____

_____

_____

_____

_____

_____

_____

_____

It looked like this:

Notes / Photos / Art

Notes / Photos / Art

Log

What I saw: _____

Date: _____

Where I saw it: _____

Observations: _____

_____

_____

_____

_____

_____

_____

_____

_____

It looked like this:

Game

With 3 or more people, gather about 20 different items from the ground and place them all in one area.

Study the items for one minute, then cover with a cloth.

Each player then lists as many items as they can remember on a piece of paper.

Uncover the items and see how many each person remembered!

59

Fact

Not all animals have blood.

Instead of using blood, sponges and flatworms use a process called diffusion to move oxygen and food throughout their bodies.

Several kinds of invertebrates (animals without spines) have blue-colored blood, and some worms have green blood.

What I saw: _____

Date: _____

Where I saw it: _____

Observations: _____

_____

_____

_____

_____

_____

_____

_____

_____

_____

It looked like this:

Index

Index

Page	Short Description
9	_____
10	_____
17	_____
18	_____
25	_____
26	_____
33	_____
34	_____
41	_____
42	_____
49	_____
50	_____
57	_____
58	_____